By the Editors of Best Recipes

Best Recipes

CAKES

COOKBOOK

Publications International, Ltd.

This edition published by Publications International, Ltd., 7373 North Cicero Avenue,
Lincolnwood, Illinois 60646.

Photography by Sacco Productions Limited/Chicago.
Photographers: Warren Hansen, Laurie Proffitt
Photo Stylists/Production: Betty Karslake, Paula Walters
Food Stylists: Lois Hlavac, Carol Parik, Moisette Sintov-McNerny

ISBN 1-56173-769-0

Pictured on the front cover: Black Forest Cake (*page 36*)

Pictured on the back cover (*counter-clockwise from top*): Lemon Dream Cheesecake (*page 92*), Brandy-
Pecan Corn Meal Cake (*page 70*), Elegant Chocolate Log (*page 28*) and Peachy Praline Cobbler Cake
(*page 56*).

Manufactured in the United States.

8 7 6 5 4 3 2 1

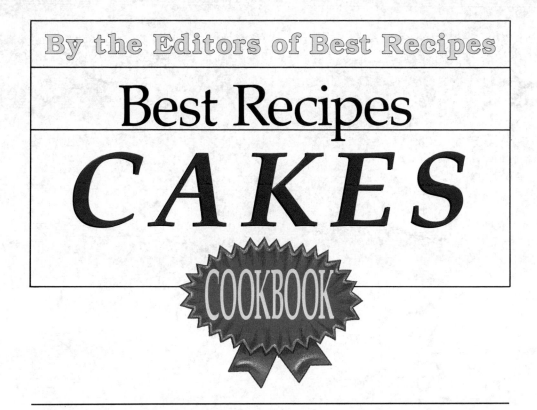

By the Editors of Best Recipes

Best Recipes

CAKES

COOKBOOK

INTRODUCTION

Nothing beats the tantalizing aroma and luscious flavor of a home-baked cake. Whether it's a light, delicate angel food cake or a decadently rich devil's food cake, many of the preparation principles remain the same. The following information on cake basics is sure to provide you with all you'll need to make your next cake presentation one that will win you raves!

The great tasting recipes in BEST RECIPES CAKES were gathered from a variety of recipe contests and bake-offs across America. Each recipe has its own mouth-watering photograph and lists the name of the winner and the contest they entered.

CAKE BASICS

Cakes are divided into two categories according to what makes them rise. Butter cakes rely primarily on baking powder or baking soda for height, while sponge cakes depend on the air trapped in the eggs during beating. Some cake recipes specifically call for cake flour which contains less protein than all-purpose flour and produces a more tender cake.

Butter Cakes

Butter cakes include pound cakes and yellow, white, spice and chocolate layer cakes. These cakes use butter, shortening or oil for moistness and richness and are leavened with baking powder and/or baking soda. Before mixing the batter, soften the butter so that it mixes easily with the sugar.

Sponge Cakes

These cakes achieve their high volume from beaten eggs rather than a leavening agent like baking powder. Sponge cakes do not contain butter, oil or shortening. Angel food cakes are the most popular and are literally fat-free since they use only egg whites, not yolks. Yellow sponge cakes are prepared with whole eggs. Chiffon cakes are also lightened with beaten eggs, but they are not true sponge cakes because they contain vegetable oil. When preparing sponge cakes, be sure to beat the eggs to the proper stage; do not overbeat or underbeat them. Handle the beaten eggs gently when folding them into the other ingredients or they will lose air and volume.

Preparing Pans

Always use the exact pan size called for in the recipe. If the pan is too large, the cake will not rise properly or brown evenly. If the pan is too small, the cake will sink in the center and the texture will be coarse; the batter may also run over the top of the pan during baking.

For butter cakes, grease and flour the pans before mixing the cake batter so that the cake can be baked immediately. To grease and flour cake pans, use a paper towel, waxed paper or your fingers to apply a thin, even layer of shortening. Sprinkle flour into the greased pan; shake or tilt the pan to coat evenly with flour, then tap lightly to remove any excess. To line pans with paper, trace the bottom of the cake pan onto a piece of waxed paper or parchment paper and cut to fit. Grease the pan, but *do not* flour it. Press the paper onto the bottom of the greased pan.

Sponge cakes are usually baked in tube pans. The center tube helps the heat circulate during baking and also supports the delicate structure of the cake. *Do not* grease the pans for sponge cakes. The ungreased pan lets the batter cling to the sides as it rises.

Baking

Place the cake pan(s) in the center of a preheated oven. Oven racks may need to be set lower for cakes baked in tube pans. If two racks are used, arrange them so they divide the oven into thirds and then stagger the pans so they are not directly over each other. Avoid opening the oven door during the first half of the baking time. The oven temperature must remain constant in order for the cake to rise properly.

A butter cake is done when it begins to pull away from the sides of the pan, the top springs back when lightly touched and a cake tester or wooden pick inserted in the center comes out clean and dry. A sponge cake is done when it is delicately browned and the top springs back when lightly touched.

Cooling

After removing butter cakes from the oven, let them stand in their pans on wire racks for 10 minutes, or as the recipe directs. Run a knife around the edge of the cake to loosen it from the sides of the pan and invert it onto a wire rack. Remove the paper liner from the cake if one was used. Turn the cake top side up onto a second rack to finish cooling. Invert a sponge cake baked in a tube pan onto a funnel or bottle immediately after removing it from the oven. If it is cooled top side up, it will fall. Do not remove a sponge cake from the pan until it is completely cool.

Frosting

Make sure the cake is completely cool before frosting it. Brush off any loose crumbs from the cake's surface. To keep the cake plate clean, place small pieces of waxed paper under the edges of the cake; remove them after the cake has been frosted. For best results, use a flat metal spatula for applying frosting. You will achieve a more professional look if you first apply a layer of thin frosting on the cake as a base coat to help seal in any remaining crumbs.

Storing

Store one-layer cakes in their baking pans, tightly covered. Store two- or three-layer cakes in a cake-saver or under a large inverted bowl. If the cake has a fluffy or cooked frosting, insert a teaspoon handle under the edge of the cover to prevent an airtight seal and moisture buildup. Cakes with whipped cream frostings or cream fillings should be stored in the refrigerator. Unfrosted cakes can be frozen for up to 4 months if well wrapped in plastic wrap. Thaw in their wrappers at room temperature. Frosted cakes should be frozen unwrapped until the frosting hardens, and then wrapped and sealed; freeze for up to 2 months. To thaw, remove the wrapping and thaw at room temperature or in the refrigerator. Cakes with fruit or custard fillings do not freeze well as they become soggy when thawed.

THE CLASSICS

Chiffon Cake

♦ Catherine A. Melvin from Edgar, Nebraska was a finalist in the Cakes category at the Nebraska State Fair, Lincoln, Nebraska.

Makes one 10-inch tube cake

  5 eggs, separated
  ½ teaspoon cream of tartar
  2¼ cups sifted all-purpose flour
  1½ cups sugar
  1 tablespoon baking powder
  1 teaspoon salt
  ¾ cup water
  ½ cup vegetable oil
  1 teaspoon vanilla
  1 teaspoon almond extract
    Strawberries, kiwifruit and whipped cream for garnish (optional)

Preheat oven to 325°F. Beat egg whites with cream of tartar at high speed with electric mixer until stiff peaks form. Set aside. Sift together dry ingredients into large bowl. Make a well in flour mixture. Add egg yolks, water, oil and flavorings; mix well. Fold in egg white mixture. Immediately pour into ungreased 10-inch tube pan. Bake 55 minutes. *Increase oven temperature to 350°F.* Continue baking 10 minutes or until cake springs back when lightly touched with finger. Invert pan and allow cake to cool completely before removing from pan. Garnish as desired.

Cherry-Pineapple Upside-Down Cake

♦ Charlotte Scott from Rock Island, Illinois was a finalist in the "Bake-a-Cake" category in the Blue Ribbon Culinary Contest at the Illinois State Fair, Springfield, Illinois.

Makes one 9-inch cake

1¼ cups sifted cake flour
  2 teaspoons baking powder
¼ teaspoon salt
½ cup (1 stick) butter or margarine, softened, divided
¾ cup granulated sugar
  1 egg, beaten
½ cup milk
  1 teaspoon vanilla
¾ cup packed brown sugar
  1 (20-ounce) can crushed pineapple, well drained
  1 (16-ounce) can sour pie cherries, drained
  Fresh mint leaves for garnish (optional)

Preheat oven to 350°F. Combine flour, baking powder and salt; set aside. Beat together ¼ cup of the butter and the granulated sugar in large bowl until light and fluffy. Blend in egg. Add flour mixture alternately with milk, beating well after each addition. Blend in vanilla. Melt the remaining ¼ cup butter in 9-inch ovenproof skillet or 9-inch cake pan. Stir in brown sugar; spread to cover bottom of skillet. Cover with pineapple. Reserve a few cherries for garnish, if desired. Spoon remaining cherries over pineapple; top with batter. Bake 50 minutes or until wooden pick inserted in center comes out clean. Cool in pan on wire rack 10 minutes. Loosen edges and turn upside down onto cake plate. Garnish with reserved cherries and mint, if desired.

Sweet Zucchini Spice Cake

♦ Sharon Norlander from Albuquerque, New Mexico was a finalist in the Cakes category at the New Mexico State Fair, Albuquerque, New Mexico.

Makes one 2-layer cake

  3 cups grated peeled zucchini (approximately
     1 pound)
  1 cup ground walnuts
  1 cup flaked coconut
  4 eggs
  1 cup vegetable oil
  2 tablespoons vanilla
2½ cups granulated sugar
  3 cups all-purpose flour
  2 teaspoons ground cinnamon
1½ teaspoons baking soda
  1 teaspoon baking powder
  1 teaspoon salt
     Pineapple Cream Cheese Icing (recipe follows)

Preheat oven to 350°F. Grease and flour 2 (10-inch) round cake pans. Combine zucchini, walnuts and coconut; set aside. Beat together eggs, oil and vanilla in large bowl until well blended. Beat in granulated sugar. Gradually add combined dry ingredients, beating well after each addition. Stir in zucchini mixture. Pour evenly into prepared pans. Bake 35 to 40 minutes or until wooden pick inserted in centers comes out clean. Cool layers in pans on wire racks 10 minutes. Loosen edges and remove to racks to cool completely. Fill and frost with Pineapple Cream Cheese Icing.

Pineapple Cream Cheese Icing: Beat together 1 (8-ounce) package softened cream cheese and ½ cup (1 stick) softened margarine in large bowl until creamy. Add 1 (8-ounce) can drained crushed pineapple. Gradually add 1 pound (approximately 4½ cups) sifted powdered sugar, beating until smooth and of spreading consistency.

Buttermilk Pound Cake

♦ Winifred Merrill from Beverly, Massachusetts was a first place winner in the Topsfield Fair Baking Competition, sponsored by the Essex Agricultural Society, Topsfield, Massachusetts.

Makes two 9×5-inch loaves

  3 cups sifted all-purpose flour
½ teaspoon baking powder
½ teaspoon baking soda
½ teaspoon salt
  1 cup (2 sticks) butter or margarine, softened
  2 cups superfine sugar
  2 eggs
  1 teaspoon vanilla
  1 teaspoon lemon extract
  1 cup buttermilk
    Starfruit and strawberry slices for garnish (optional)
    Lemon or orange zest for garnish (optional)

Preheat oven to 350°F. Grease and flour 2 (9×5-inch) loaf pans. Combine flour, baking powder, baking soda and salt; set aside. Beat together butter and sugar in large bowl until light and fluffy. Add eggs, one at a time, beating well after each addition. Blend in flavorings. Add flour mixture alternately with buttermilk, beating well after each addition. Pour evenly into prepared pans. Bake 35 to 40 minutes or until wooden pick inserted in centers comes out clean. Cool loaves in pans on wire racks 10 minutes. Loosen edges and remove to racks to cool completely. Garnish as desired.

Burnt Sugar Cake

♦ Eileen Darby from Albuquerque, New Mexico was a finalist in the Cakes category at the New Mexico State Fair, Albuquerque, New Mexico.

Makes one 2-layer cake

1½ cups granulated sugar, divided
½ cup boiling water
2 eggs, separated
½ cup (1 stick) margarine, softened
1 teaspoon vanilla
2¼ cups all-purpose flour
1 tablespoon baking powder
1 teaspoon salt
1 cup milk
Caramel Frosting (recipe follows)

Heat ½ cup of the granulated sugar in heavy 8-inch skillet over medium heat, stirring constantly, until sugar is melted and golden brown. Remove from heat; reduce heat to low. Gradually stir in boiling water; continue cooking until sugar is dissolved, stirring constantly. If necessary, add enough water to syrup to measure ½ cup; cool.

Preheat oven to 375°F. Grease and flour 2 (8-inch) round cake pans. Beat egg whites at medium speed with electric mixer until foamy. Gradually add ½ cup of the remaining granulated sugar, beating at high speed until stiff beaks form. *(Do not underbeat.)* Set aside. Beat together margarine and the remaining ½ cup granulated sugar in large bowl until light and fluffy. Beat in egg yolks. Blend in vanilla. Gradually add sugar syrup, mixing until well blended. Add combined dry ingredients alternately with milk, beating well after each addition. Fold in egg white mixture. Pour evenly into prepared pans. Bake 20 to 25 minutes or until wooden pick inserted in centers comes out clean. Cool layers in pans on wire racks 10 minutes. Loosen edges and remove to racks to cool completely. Fill and frost with Caramel Frosting. Garnish as desired.

Caramel Frosting: Melt 2 tablespoons margarine in 2-quart saucepan. Stir in ⅔ cup packed brown sugar, ⅛ teaspoon salt and ⅓ cup evaporated milk. Bring to a boil, stirring constantly. Remove from heat; cool to lukewarm. Beat in 2½ cups powdered sugar until frosting is of spreading consistency. Blend in ½ teaspoon vanilla.

Boston Cream Pie

♦ Sarah Cuozzo from Boxford, Massachusetts was a first place winner in the Topsfield Fair Baking Competition, sponsored by the Essex Agricultural Society, Topsfield, Massachusetts.

Makes one 9-inch cake

⅓ **cup shortening**
1 **cup granulated sugar**
1 **egg**
1 **teaspoon vanilla**
1¼ **cups all-purpose flour**
1½ **teaspoons baking powder**
½ **teaspoon salt**
¾ **cup milk**
   Filling (recipe follows)
   Glaze (recipe follows)

Preheat oven to 350°F. Grease and flour 1 (9-inch) round cake pan. Beat together shortening and sugar in large bowl until light and fluffy. Blend in egg and vanilla. Add combined dry ingredients to sugar mixture alternately with milk, beating well after each addition. Pour into prepared pan. Bake 35 minutes or until wooden pick inserted in center comes out clean. Cool in pan 10 minutes. Loosen edges and remove to rack to cool completely. When cool, split cake horizontally in half to make 2 thin layers. To assemble, spoon Filling over bottom half of cake on cake plate; cover with top half of cake layer. Spread top with Glaze; let cool. Serve when glaze is completely set. Refrigerate.

Filling: Combine ⅓ cup granulated sugar, 2 tablespoons cornstarch and ¼ teaspoon salt in 2-quart saucepan. Gradually stir in 1½ cups milk. Cook over medium heat, stirring constantly, until mixture thickens and comes to boil. Boil 1 minute, stirring constantly. Gradually stir small amount of hot mixture into 2 slightly beaten egg yolks; mix thoroughly. Return to hot mixture in pan. Return to boil; boil 1 minute, stirring constantly. *(Do not overcook.)* Remove from heat; stir in 2 teaspoons vanilla. Cool to room temperature. Chill.

Glaze: Combine 2 (1-ounce) squares unsweetened chocolate and 3 tablespoons butter in medium saucepan; stir over low heat until melted. Remove from heat; stir in 1 cup powdered sugar and ¾ teaspoon vanilla. Stir in 1 to 2 tablespoons water, a teaspoonful at a time, until glaze is of desired consistency. Cool slightly.

White Buttermilk Cake

♦ Inez Mortley from Albuquerque, New Mexico was a finalist in the Cakes category at the New Mexico State Fair, Albuquerque, New Mexico.

Makes one 2- or 3-layer cake

3 cups sifted cake flour
1 teaspoon baking soda
½ teaspoon salt
1 cup shortening
2 cups granulated sugar, divided
1 cup buttermilk
2 teaspoons clear vanilla
½ teaspoon almond extract
6 egg whites, at room temperature
1 teaspoon cream of tartar
Creamy Frosting (recipe follows)

Preheat oven to 350°F. Grease and flour 2 (9-inch) or 3 (8-inch) round cake pans. Combine flour, baking soda and salt; set aside. Beat together shortening with 1⅓ cups of the granulated sugar in large bowl until light and fluffy. Add flour mixture alternately with buttermilk, beating well after each addition. Blend in flavorings. Beat egg whites in separate bowl at medium speed with electric mixer until foamy. Add cream of tartar; beat at high speed until soft peaks form. Gradually beat in the remaining ⅔ cup granulated sugar, beating until stiff peaks form; fold into flour mixture. Pour evenly into prepared pans. Bake 30 to 35 minutes or until wooden pick inserted in centers comes out clean. Cool layers in pans on wire racks 10 minutes. Loosen edges and remove to racks to cool completely. Fill and frost with Creamy Frosting.

Creamy Frosting: Combine 3 tablespoons all-purpose flour and 1 cup milk in medium saucepan; stir over low heat until thickened. Cool. Beat 1 cup (2 sticks) softened butter in large bowl until creamy. Add 1 cup powdered sugar; beat until fluffy. Blend in 1 teaspoon vanilla. Add flour mixture; beat until thick and smooth.

Carrot Cake

♦ Eileen McClafferty from Central Islip, New York was a third place winner in the POLLY-O® International Recipe Competition, Mineola, New York.

Makes one 10-inch tube cake

- **1 cup granulated sugar**
- **1 cup packed brown sugar**
- **1 cup vegetable oil**
- **1 cup POLLY-O® Ricotta Cheese**
- **3 eggs**
- **2 cups all-purpose flour**
- **2 teaspoons baking powder**
- **2 teaspoons baking soda**
- **1 teaspoon salt**
- **2 teaspoons ground cinnamon**
- **½ teaspoon ground nutmeg**
- **2 cups shredded carrots (approximately 1½ pounds)**
- **½ cup chopped pineapple***
- **¼ to ½ cup raisins**
- **½ cup chopped walnuts**
  Cream Cheese Topping (recipe follows)
  Additional raisins and chopped walnuts for garnish (optional)

Preheat oven to 350°F. Grease and flour 10-inch tube pan. Beat together sugars, oil and ricotta cheese in large bowl until light and fluffy. Add eggs, one at a time, beating well after each addition. Sift together dry ingredients; gradually add to sugar mixture, mixing until well blended. Stir in carrots, fruit and walnuts. Pour into prepared pan, spreading evenly to edges. Bake 1 hour or until wooden pick inserted in center comes out clean. Cool in pan on wire rack 10 minutes. Loosen edges and remove to rack to cool completely. Refrigerate. Top with Cream Cheese Topping just before serving. Garnish as desired.

Cream Cheese Topping: Beat together 2 tablespoons softened butter, 4 ounces softened cream cheese, ½ cup POLLY-O® Ricotta Cheese and 1 teaspoon vanilla until well blended. Add 2 cups powdered sugar; beat until smooth and creamy.

If using canned pineapple, use drained unsweetened pineapple.

Note: *To help prevent raisins from sinking in cake batter, toss raisins lightly with small amount of flour before adding to batter.*

Angel Food Cake

◆ Nancy Turner from St. Clair Shores, Michigan was a prize winner in the Cakes category at the Michigan State Fair, Detroit, Michigan.

Makes one 10-inch tube cake

1¼ cups cake flour, sifted
1⅓ cups plus ½ cup sugar, divided
12 egg whites
1¼ teaspoons cream of tartar
¼ teaspoon salt
1 teaspoon vanilla
¼ teaspoon almond extract
Fresh strawberries for serving (optional)

Preheat oven to 350°F. Sift together flour with ½ cup of the sugar 4 times. Beat egg whites with cream of tartar, salt and flavorings in large bowl at high speed with electric mixer until stiff peaks form. Gradually add the remaining 1⅓ cups sugar, mixing well after each addition. Fold in flour mixture. Pour into ungreased 10-inch tube pan. Bake 35 to 40 minutes or until cake springs back when lightly touched with finger. Invert pan and allow cake to cool completely in pan before removing from pan. Serve with strawberries, if desired.

Lady Baltimore Cake

♦ Omadeane Talley from Lincoln, Nebraska was a first place winner in the Lady Baltimore Cakes division at the Nebraska State Fair, Lincoln, Nebraska.

Makes one 3-layer cake

1¼ cups shortening
2¼ cups sugar
 2 teaspoons vanilla
3¼ cups all-purpose flour
4½ teaspoons baking powder
1½ teaspoons salt
1½ cups milk
 8 egg whites, at room temperature
 Filling (recipe follows)
 Frosting (recipe follows)

Preheat oven to 350°F. Grease 3 (9-inch) round cake pans; cover bottoms with waxed paper. Beat together shortening and sugar in large bowl until light and fluffy. Blend in vanilla. Sift together dry ingredients. Add to sugar mixture alternately with milk, beating well after each addition. Beat egg whites in separate bowl at high speed with electric mixer until stiff peaks form; fold into batter. Pour evenly into prepared pans. Bake 30 minutes or until wooden pick inserted in centers comes out clean. Cool layers in pans on wire racks 10 minutes. Loosen edges and remove to racks to cool completely. To assemble, spread 2 cake layers with Filling; stack on cake plate. Top with remaining cake layer. Frost with Frosting.

Filling: Melt ½ cup (1 stick) butter or margarine in 2-quart saucepan. Stir in 1 cup sugar, ⅓ cup bourbon *or* brandy and ½ cup water. Bring to a boil, stirring occasionally to dissolve sugar. Stir small amount of hot mixture into 10 slightly beaten egg yolks; return to hot mixture in saucepan. Cook until thickened. Remove from heat; stir in 1 cup finely chopped raisins, ¾ cup chopped pecans, ½ cup drained chopped maraschino cherries and ½ cup flaked coconut. Blend in ¾ teaspoon vanilla. Cool completely.

Frosting: Combine 1½ cups sugar, ½ cup water, 2 egg whites,* 2 teaspoons corn syrup *or* ¼ teaspoon cream of tartar, and dash of salt in top of double boiler. Beat 30 seconds. Place on top of range; cook, stirring occasionally, over simmering water 7 minutes. Remove from heat; add 1 teaspoon vanilla. Beat 3 minutes or until frosting is of spreading consistency.

Use clean, uncracked eggs.

THE CHOCOLATE COLLECTION

Devil's Food Cake with Ricotta Frosting

♦ Margaret A. Cyrus from New Orleans, Louisiana was a finalist in a cookbook and recipe contest sponsored by *The Times-Picayune*, New Orleans, Louisiana.

Makes one 2-layer cake

- **1 cup shortening**
- **3 cups granulated sugar**
- **3 eggs**
- **2 cups buttermilk**
- **1 teaspoon baking soda**
- **3 cups all-purpose flour**
- **6 tablespoons cocoa**
- **1½ teaspoons ground cinnamon**
- **¼ teaspoon ground cloves**
- **1 tablespoon vanilla**
- **Ricotta Frosting (recipe follows)**

Preheat oven to 350°F. Grease and flour 2 (9-inch) square baking pans. Beat together shortening and granulated sugar in large bowl until light and fluffy. Add eggs, one at a time, beating well after each addition. Gradually add buttermilk to soda, mixing well. Sift together flour, cocoa and spices; add to egg mixture alternately with buttermilk mixture, beating well after each addition. Blend in vanilla. Pour evenly into prepared pans. Bake 25 minutes or until wooden pick inserted in centers comes out clean. Cool layers in pans on wire racks 10 minutes. Loosen edges and remove to racks to cool completely. Fill and frost with Ricotta Frosting.

Ricotta Frosting: Beat together 2½ pounds ricotta cheese, 1 teaspoon almond extract and 1½ cups powdered sugar until smooth. Add 1 finely chopped (8-ounce) chocolate bar with almonds; mix well.

Elegant Chocolate Log

♦ Bobbie Mellulis from Greenville, Illinois was a finalist in the "Bake-a-Cake" category in the Blue Ribbon Culinary Contest at the Illinois State Fair, Springfield, Illinois.

Makes one log

3¼ cups sifted powdered sugar, divided
  5 tablespoons sifted all-purpose flour
  ½ teaspoon salt
  5 tablespoons cocoa
  6 eggs, separated
  ¼ teaspoon cream of tartar
1¼ teaspoons vanilla
  1 tablespoon water
  1 cup whipping cream
  2 tablespoons granulated sugar
12 large marshmallows, cut up, *or* ¾ cup miniature
      marshmallows
  1 (1-ounce) square unsweetened chocolate, melted,
      cooled
  3 to 4 tablespoons light cream, half and half, or milk
  ¼ cup chopped pecans

Preheat oven to 375°F. Grease 15×10×1-inch jelly roll pan; line with waxed paper. Sift together 1¾ cups of the powdered sugar, the flour, salt and cocoa 3 times; set aside. Beat egg whites at high speed with electric mixer until foamy. Add cream of tartar; beat until stiff peaks form. Set aside. Beat egg yolks in separate large bowl at high speed with electric mixer until thick and lemon-colored. Blend in vanilla and water. Add dry ingredients; beat on medium speed until well blended. Fold in egg whites. Spread into prepared pan. Bake 15 to 20 minutes or until wooden pick inserted in center comes out clean. Meanwhile, lightly dust clean dish towel with additional powdered sugar. Loosen warm cake from edges of pan with spatula; invert onto towel. Remove pan; carefully peel off paper. Cut off crisp edges with sharp knife. Roll up cake gently, from narrow end, by folding cake over and then tucking it in towel. Continue rolling cake, using towel as an aid. Let cake cool completely in towel on wire rack. Beat whipping cream in separate small bowl at high speed with electric mixer until thickened. Gradually add granulated sugar, beating until soft peaks form. Fold in marshmallows. Unroll cake; remove towel. Spread with whipped cream mixture; reroll cake. Combine cooled chocolate and the remaining 1½ cups powdered sugar. Stir in light cream, a tablespoonful at a time, until frosting is spreading consistency. Spread over cake roll; sprinkle with pecans. Refrigerate.

Chocolate Praline Layer Cake

♦ Julie Konecne from Bemidji, Minnesota was a Grand Prize winner at the Pillsbury BAKE-OFF® Contest in San Diego, California.

Makes one 2-layer cake

½ cup (1 stick) butter or margarine
¼ cup whipping cream
1 cup packed brown sugar
¾ cup coarsely chopped pecans
1 (18.25-ounce) package PILLSBURY® Plus Devil's Food Cake Mix
1¼ cups water
⅓ cup vegetable oil
3 eggs
Topping (recipe follows)
Pecan halves and chocolate curls for garnish (optional)

Preheat oven to 325°F. Grease 2 (8- or 9-inch) round cake pans. Combine butter, whipping cream and brown sugar in small heavy saucepan. Cook over low heat just until butter is melted, stirring occasionally. Pour evenly into prepared pans; sprinkle evenly with chopped pecans. Combine cake mix, water, oil and eggs in large bowl; beat at low speed until moistened, then beat at high speed 2 minutes. Carefully spoon batter over praline mixture in pans. Bake 35 minutes or until cake springs back when lightly touched with finger. Cool layers in pans on wire racks 10 minutes. Loosen edges and remove to racks to cool completely. To assemble, place 1 layer, praline side up, on cake plate. Spread with half of the Topping. Top with the second layer, praline side up; spread with remaining topping. Refrigerate. Garnish as desired.

Topping: Beat 1¾ cups whipping cream in small bowl at medium speed with electric mixer until soft peaks form. Blend in ¼ cup powdered sugar and ¼ teaspoon vanilla; beat at high speed until stiff peaks form.

Chocolate Angel Food Cake

♦ Jeanette Monahan from Albuquerque, New Mexico was a finalist in the Cakes category at the New Mexico State Fair, Albuquerque, New Mexico.

Makes one 10-inch tube cake

1½ cups granulated sugar, divided
¾ cup sifted cake flour
¼ cup cocoa
¼ teaspoon salt
12 egg whites
1½ teaspoons cream of tartar
1½ teaspoons vanilla
   Powdered sugar for garnish (optional)

Preheat oven to 375°F. Sift together ¾ cup of the granulated sugar with the flour, cocoa and salt 2 times; set aside. Beat egg whites in large bowl at medium speed with electric mixer until foamy. Add cream of tartar; beat at high speed until soft peaks form. Gradually add the remaining ¾ cup granulated sugar, 2 tablespoons at a time, beating until stiff peaks form. Blend in vanilla. Sift about one fourth of the cocoa mixture over egg white mixture; fold in. Repeat with remaining cocoa mixture. Pour into ungreased 10-inch tube pan. Bake 35 to 40 minutes or until cake springs back when lightly touched with finger. Invert pan and allow cake to cool completely before removing from pan. Turn cake onto cake plate. Dust lightly with powdered sugar just before serving, if desired. Garnish as desired.

Zucchini Chocolate Cake

♦ Mrs. Val Sypal from Brainard, Nebraska was a finalist in the Zucchini Cakes category at the Nebraska State Fair, Lincoln, Nebraska.

Makes one 13×9-inch cake

½ cup (1 stick) margarine or butter, softened
½ cup vegetable oil
1⅔ cups granulated sugar
2 eggs
1 teaspoon vanilla
½ teaspoon chocolate flavoring
2½ cups all-purpose flour
¼ cup cocoa
1 teaspoon baking soda
½ teaspoon salt
½ cup buttermilk
2 cups shredded zucchini
1 (6-ounce) package semisweet chocolate chips
½ cup chopped nuts

Preheat oven to 325°F. Grease and lightly flour 13×9-inch baking pan. Beat together margarine, oil and sugar in large bowl until light and fluffy. Add eggs, one at a time, beating well after each addition. Blend in flavorings. Combine dry ingredients. Add to creamed mixture alternately with buttermilk, beating well after each addition. Stir in zucchini. Pour into prepared pan. Sprinkle with chocolate chips and nuts. Bake 55 minutes or until wooden pick inserted in center comes out clean; cool on wire rack. Cut into squares. Frost with your favorite chocolate frosting, if desired.

Black Forest Cake

♦ Lynn Morford from Sherman, Illinois was a finalist in the "Bake-a-Cake" category in the Blue Ribbon Culinary Contest at the Illinois State Fair, Springfield, Illinois.

Makes one 3-layer cake

  2 cups plus 2 tablespoons all-purpose flour
1½ teaspoons baking powder
  ¾ teaspoon baking soda
  ¾ teaspoon salt
  2 cups granulated sugar
  ¾ cup cocoa
  3 eggs
  1 cup milk
  ½ cup vegetable oil
  1 tablespoon vanilla
    Cherry Topping (recipe follows)
    Frosting (recipe follows)

Preheat oven to 350°F. Grease and flour 2 (9-inch) round cake pans. Cover bottoms with waxed paper. Combine dry ingredients in large bowl. Add eggs, milk, oil and vanilla; beat until well blended. Pour evenly into prepared pans. Bake 35 minutes or until wooden pick inserted in centers comes out clean. Cool layers in pans on wire racks 10 minutes. Loosen edges and remove to racks to cool completely. While cake is baking, prepare Cherry Topping; cool. Split cooled cakes horizontally in half to make 4 layers. Tear 1 layer into crumbs; set aside. Reserve 1½ cups Frosting for decorating cake; set aside. To assemble, place 1 layer on cake plate. Spread with 1 cup frosting; top with ¾ cup cherry topping. Top with second cake layer; repeat layers of frosting and cherry topping. Top with third cake layer. Frost sides of cake with remaining frosting. Pat reserved crumbs into frosting on sides of cake; pipe reserved 1½ cups frosting around top and bottom edges of cake. Spoon remaining cherry topping onto top of cake. Refrigerate.

Cherry Topping: Drain 2 (20-ounce) cans tart pitted cherries, reserving ½ cup juice. Combine reserved juice, cherries, 1 cup granulated sugar and ¼ cup cornstarch in 2-quart saucepan. Cook over low heat until thickened, stirring constantly. Stir in 1 teaspoon vanilla. Cool; set aside.

Frosting: Beat together 3 cups whipping cream and ⅓ cup powdered sugar in chilled bowl at high speed with electric mixer until stiff peaks form.

Tin Roof Sundae Cake

♦ Elinor Commander from Ponce de Leon, Florida was a Grand Prize/First Place winner in the Cakes category in the Recipe Contest at the National Peanut Festival, Dothan, Alabama.

Makes one 3-layer cake

> 1 cup (2 sticks) butter, softened
> 2 cups granulated sugar
> 4 eggs
> 3 cups all-purpose flour
> 2 teaspoons baking powder
> 1 cup milk
> 1 teaspoon *each* vanilla and butter flavoring
> 3 tablespoons cocoa
> Filling (recipe follows)
> Frosting (recipe follows)
> Melted white chocolate for garnish (optional)

Preheat oven to 350°F. Grease and flour 3 (8- to 9-inch) round cake pans. Beat together butter and sugar in large bowl until light and fluffy. Add eggs, one at a time, beating well after each addition. Combine flour and baking powder. Add to butter mixture alternately with milk, beating well after each addition. Blend in flavorings. Pour one third of the batter into *each of* 2 of the prepared pans. Blend cocoa into the remaining batter; pour into remaining pan. Bake 30 minutes or until wooden pick inserted in centers comes out clean. Cool layers in pans on wire racks 10 minutes. Loosen edges and remove to racks to cool completely. To assemble, place 1 yellow layer on cake plate; spread with half of the Filling. Cover with chocolate layer; spread with remaining filling. Top with remaining layer. Frost with Frosting. Garnish as desired.

Filling: Beat together ½ cup (1 stick) softened butter and 4 ounces softened cream cheese in medium bowl until creamy. Gradually add 2 cups powdered sugar, beating until fluffy. Blend in ¾ cup crunchy peanut butter, 1 teaspoon vanilla and 1 teaspoon butter flavoring. Stir in ⅓ cup finely chopped peanuts. (Add 1 to 2 tablespoons milk if necessary for desired consistency.)

Frosting: Beat together 4 ounces softened cream cheese and ¼ cup (½ stick) softened butter in medium bowl until creamy. Beat in 1 egg yolk.* Blend in 2 (1-ounce) squares melted unsweetened chocolate, 1 tablespoon lemon juice and 1 teaspoon vanilla. Gradually beat in 2 cups powdered sugar until fluffy.

*Use clean, uncracked egg.

Chocolate Yogurt Cake

♦ Mrs. George Hulett from Shively, Kentucky was a finalist in the Cakes category at the Kentucky State Fair, Louisville, Kentucky.

Makes one 2-layer cake

⅔ cup shortening
1¾ cups granulated sugar
2 eggs
1 teaspoon Cognac vanilla or vanilla
2½ cups sifted cake flour
1½ teaspoons baking soda
½ teaspoon salt
1 cup (8 ounces) plain yogurt
½ cup boiling water
½ cup cocoa
  Filling (recipe follows)
  Fluffy Cocoa Frosting (recipe follows)
  Additional chopped hazelnuts for garnish (optional)
  Toasted flaked coconut for garnish (optional)

Preheat oven to 350°F. Grease and flour 2 (9-inch) round cake pans. Beat together shortening and sugar until light and fluffy. Add eggs, one at a time, beating well after each addition. Blend in vanilla. Combine flour, baking soda and salt. Add to shortening mixture alternately with yogurt, beating well after each addition. Gradually add boiling water to cocoa, stirring until well blended; cool slightly. Add to batter; beat until well blended. Pour evenly into prepared pans. Bake 35 minutes or until wooden pick inserted in centers comes out clean. Cool layers in pans on wire racks 10 minutes. Loosen edges and remove to racks to cool completely. To assemble, place 1 cake layer on cake plate; spread with Filling. Top with second cake layer. Frost with Fluffy Cocoa Frosting. Garnish as desired.

Filling: Combine ½ cup Fluffy Cocoa Frosting (recipe follows), 2 tablespoons chopped frozen cherries, thawed, ¼ cup flaked coconut and ¼ cup chopped toasted hazelnuts, mixing until well blended.

Fluffy Cocoa Frosting: Combine 4 cups powdered sugar and ¾ cup cocoa; set aside. Beat ½ cup (1 stick) softened unsalted butter in large bowl until creamy. Add half of the cocoa mixture; beat until fluffy. Blend in ¼ cup evaporated milk and 1 teaspoon Cognac vanilla or vanilla. Gradually add the remaining powdered sugar mixture, beating until well blended. Add additional ¼ cup evaporated milk; beat until frosting is of spreading consistency. (Additional evaporated milk may be added, if desired, for a softer frosting.)

FULL-O-FRUIT CAKES

Date Torte

♦ Hilda Holvat from Palm Springs, California was a finalist in a baking contest held at the National Date Festival, Indio, California.

Makes one 2-layer cake

>   **Chocolate Nut Filling (recipe follows)**
> ½ **pound pitted dates (about 1 cup)**
> 9 **egg whites**
> 2 **cups sifted powdered sugar**
> 2 **cups coarsely ground almonds**
> 2 **tablespoons dry bread crumbs**
>   **Additional powdered sugar for garnish (optional)**

Prepare Chocolate Nut Filling; chill until ready to use. Preheat oven to 350°F. Grease and flour 2 (9-inch) round cake pans. Reserve a few dates for garnish, if desired; coarsely chop remaining dates. Beat egg whites in large bowl at medium speed with electric mixer until foamy. Gradually add sugar, beating at high speed until stiff peaks form. Stir together almonds and bread crumbs; fold into egg white mixture. Fold in chopped dates. Pour evenly into prepared pans. Bake 25 to 30 minutes or until lightly browned. Cool layers in pans on wire racks 10 minutes. Loosen edges and remove to racks to cool completely. To assemble, place 1 layer on cake plate; spread with filling. Cover with second layer. Dust lightly with additional powdered sugar just before serving and garnish with reserved dates, if desired.

Chocolate Nut Filling: Beat together ½ cup (1 stick) softened butter and 1 cup sifted powdered sugar in medium bowl until light and fluffy. Blend in 1 (1-ounce) square melted semisweet chocolate. Stir in ½ cup coarsely ground almonds.

Banana Cake

♦ Mary Foster from Sandia Park, New Mexico was a finalist in the Cakes category at the New Mexico State Fair, Albuquerque, New Mexico.

Makes one 2-layer cake

2½ cups all-purpose flour
 1 teaspoon salt
 ¾ teaspoon baking powder
 ¾ teaspoon baking soda
 ⅔ cup shortening
1⅔ cups sugar
 2 eggs
1¼ cups mashed ripe bananas (2 to 3 medium bananas)
 ⅔ cup buttermilk, divided
 ⅔ cup chopped walnuts
    Frosting (recipe follows)

Preheat oven to 375°F. Grease and flour 2 (9-inch) round cake pans. Combine flour, salt, baking powder and baking soda; set aside. Beat together shortening and sugar in large bowl until light and fluffy. Add eggs, one at a time, beating well after each addition. Blend in bananas. Add flour mixture alternately with buttermilk, beating well after each addition. Stir in walnuts. Pour evenly into prepared pans. Bake 30 to 35 minutes or until wooden pick inserted in centers comes out clean. Cool layers in pans on wire racks 10 minutes. Loosen edges and remove to racks to cool completely. Fill and frost with Frosting.

Frosting: Combine ⅓ cup plus 2 tablespoons all-purpose flour and dash of salt in 2-quart saucepan. Gradually stir in 1 cup milk until well blended. Cook over medium heat until thickened, stirring constantly. Cool. Beat together ½ cup shortening and ½ cup (1 stick) softened margarine in large bowl until creamy. Add 1¼ cups granulated sugar; beat until light and fluffy. Blend in 1 teaspoon vanilla. Add cooled flour mixture; beat until smooth.

Apple Upside-Down Cake

♦ May Kuckro from Wethersfield, Connecticut was a prize winner in the tenth- to twelfth-grade category in the Apple Recipe Contest for Grades 5 to 12, sponsored by *The Hartford Courant*, Hartford, Connecticut.

Makes one 8-inch cake

¼ cup (½ stick) plus 3 tablespoons butter, divided
½ cup packed brown sugar
½ teaspoon ground cinnamon
¼ teaspoon ground nutmeg
¼ teaspoon ground mace
3 McIntosh apples, peeled, cored and sliced into thin rings*
2 teaspoons lemon juice
1⅓ cups cake flour
¾ cup granulated sugar
1¾ teaspoons baking powder
¼ teaspoon salt
½ cup milk
1 teaspoon vanilla
1 egg, separated

Preheat oven to 375°F. Melt ¼ cup of the butter in 8-inch square pan. Add brown sugar and spices; mix well. Arrange apple slices over brown sugar mixture in bottom of pan; sprinkle with lemon juice. Set aside. Combine dry ingredients in large bowl. Add the remaining 3 tablespoons butter; cut with pastry blender until mixture resembles coarse crumbs. Add milk and vanilla; beat at low speed with electric mixer until dry ingredients are moistened. Continue beating 2 minutes at medium speed. Blend in egg yolk. Beat egg white in separate bowl at high speed with electric mixer until stiff peaks form; gently fold into batter. Pour over apples in pan. Bake 35 minutes or until wooden pick inserted in center comes out clean. Cool in pan on wire rack 5 minutes. Loosen edges and invert onto serving plate. Let stand 1 minute before removing pan. Serve warm.

Substitute any large cooking apples for McIntosh apples.

Spanish Orange-Almond Cake

♦ Marilyn Bernhardt from Springfield, Illinois was a finalist in the "Bake-a-Cake" category in the Blue Ribbon Culinary Contest at the Illinois State Fair, Springfield, Illinois.

Makes one 8-inch or 9-inch cake

⅓ cup shortening
1 cup plus 2 tablespoons sugar, divided
1 egg
1¼ cups all-purpose flour
1½ teaspoons baking powder
½ teaspoon salt
¾ cup milk
4 teaspoons grated orange peel
½ cup sliced almonds
¼ cup orange-flavored liqueur
Orange zest for garnish (optional)

Preheat oven to 350°F. Grease and flour 8-inch square or 9-inch round cake pan. Beat together shortening and 1 cup of the sugar in large bowl until light and fluffy. Add egg; beat until well blended. Combine flour, baking powder and salt. Add to sugar mixture alternately with milk, beating well after each addition. Stir in orange peel. Pour into prepared pan; sprinkle with almonds. Bake 40 to 45 minutes or until wooden pick inserted in center comes out clean. Sprinkle with the remaining 2 tablespoons sugar; drizzle with liqueur. Cool in pan on wire rack 10 minutes. Loosen edges and remove to rack to cool completely. Serve almond side up. Garnish as desired.

Fresh Pear Cake

♦ Adeline Ulibarri from Santa Fe, New Mexico was a finalist in the Cakes category at the New Mexico State Fair, Albuquerque, New Mexico.

Makes one 10-inch tube cake

4 cups chopped peeled pears
2 cups granulated sugar
1 cup chopped nuts
2 eggs
1 cup vegetable oil
1 teaspoon vanilla
3 cups all-purpose flour
2 teaspoons baking soda
½ teaspoon salt
½ teaspoon ground cinnamon
½ teaspoon ground nutmeg
Powdered sugar for garnish, if desired (optional)

Preheat oven to 375°F. Grease and flour 10-inch fluted tube or tube pan. Combine pears, granulated sugar and nuts; mix lightly. Let stand 1 hour, stirring frequently. Combine flour, baking soda, salt and spices; set aside. Beat eggs in large bowl. Blend in oil and vanilla. Add flour mixture; mix well. Stir in pear mixture. Pour into prepared pan, spreading evenly to edges. Bake 1 hour and 15 minutes or until wooden pick inserted in center comes out clean. Cool in pan on wire rack 10 minutes. Loosen edges and remove to rack to cool completely. Dust lightly with powdered sugar just before serving, if desired.

Seedy Lemon Cake

◆ Mrs. Ted Erbele from Lehr, North Dakota was a finalist in the Sunflower Council Recipe Contest sponsored by the National Sunflower Association, Bismarck, North Dakota.

Makes two 9×5-inch loaves

1½ cups sugar
   Grated peel of 2 lemons
 1 cup sunflower oil
 6 eggs
1⅔ cups plus 1 tablespoon all-purpose flour, divided
 2 teaspoons baking powder
 ¼ teaspoon salt
 ½ cup sunflower kernels
   Whipped cream and lemon zest for garnish
   (optional)

Preheat oven to 300°F. Grease and flour 2 (9×5-inch) loaf pans. Beat together sugar, lemon peel and oil in large bowl. Add eggs, one at a time, beating well after each addition. Add 1⅔ cups of the flour, the baking powder and salt; mix well. Combine the remaining 1 tablespoon flour and the sunflower kernels; toss lightly. Stir into batter. Pour evenly into prepared pans. Bake 1 hour or until wooden pick inserted in centers comes out clean. Cool loaves in pans on wire racks 10 minutes. Loosen edges and remove to racks to cool completely. Garnish as desired.

Punch Bowl Cake

♦ Tracy Crouch from Harding Academy, Searcy, Arkansas was a prize winner in a contest run by home economics teachers across the United States, sponsored by the Cherry Marketing Institute, Inc., Okemos, Michigan.

Makes one cake

1 (18.25-ounce) package butter cake mix with pudding, *plus* ingredients to prepare the mix
1 (6-ounce) package vanilla flavor instant pudding and pie filling mix, *plus* ingredients to prepare the mix
1 (20-ounce) can crushed pineapple, undrained, divided
2 (21-ounce) cans cherry pie filling, divided
1 (12-ounce) container frozen whipped topping, thawed, divided
½ cup chopped nuts, divided

Prepare and bake cake mix according to package directions; cool completely. Prepare pudding mix according to package directions. Crumble half of the cake into bottom of large bowl. (A small punch bowl works well.) Top with layers of half of the pudding, pineapple, cherry pie filling, whipped topping and nuts. (If desired, reserve a few cherries from second can of cherry pie filling for garnish.) Repeat layers, using the remaining cake, pudding, pineapple, cherry pie filling and nuts. Top with the remaining whipped topping. Garnish with reserved cherries, if desired.

Peachy Praline Cobbler Cake

♦ Karen Stephens from Hamden, Connecticut was a first place winner in the Dessert category in the "PHILLY"® Hall of Fame Recipe Contest sponsored by PHILADELPHIA BRAND® Cream Cheese, Glenview, Illinois.

Makes one 9-inch cake

1 (8-ounce) package PHILADELPHIA BRAND®
    Cream Cheese, softened
1 cup packed brown sugar
4 eggs, beaten
½ cup half and half
1 teaspoon vanilla
1 cup graham cracker crumbs
1 (6-ounce) package almond brickle chips
½ cup chopped pecans, toasted
½ cup BAKER'S® ANGEL FLAKE® Coconut
1 (16-ounce) can sliced peaches, well drained,
    chopped
1 cup whipping cream, whipped, for garnish
    (optional)
    Additional peach slices for garnish (optional)
    Fresh mint leaves for garnish (optional)

Preheat oven to 350°F. Grease 9-inch square baking pan. Beat together cream cheese and sugar in large bowl until well blended. Add eggs, one at a time, beating well after each addition. Blend in half and half and vanilla. Add crumbs, chips, pecans and coconut; mix well. Stir in peaches. Pour into prepared pan. Bake 35 to 40 minutes or until firm and edges are golden brown. Serve warm or chilled. Garnish as desired.

Blueberry Cake

♦ Cathy Demetrio from Evanston, Illinois was a finalist in the "Bake-a-Cake" category in the Blue Ribbon Culinary Contest at the Illinois State Fair, Springfield, Illinois.

Makes one 9-inch cake

½ cup (1 stick) butter, softened
⅔ cup sugar, divided
1 egg, beaten
2½ teaspoons vanilla, divided
1½ cups all-purpose flour
1½ teaspoons baking powder
4 cups fresh blueberries
2 cups sour cream
2 egg yolks
¼ teaspoon ground cardamom
¼ teaspoon grated lemon peel
Lemon zest and fresh mint leaves for garnish (optional)

Preheat oven to 350°F. Grease 9-inch springform pan. Beat together butter and ⅓ cup of the sugar in large bowl until light and fluffy. Blend in beaten egg and 1½ teaspoons of the vanilla. Sift together flour and baking powder. Add to butter mixture, mixing until well blended. Spread onto bottom of prepared pan; cover with blueberries. Combine the remaining ⅓ cup sugar, the remaining 1 teaspoon vanilla, the sour cream, egg yolks, cardamom and lemon peel; pour over blueberries. Bake 50 to 55 minutes or until set. (*Do not overbake.*) Cool 10 minutes. Loosen cake from rim of pan; cool completely before removing rim of pan. Garnish as desired.

Apple-Nut Cinnamon Streusel Cake

♦ Ester Heinle from Hebron, North Dakota was a finalist in the Sunflower Council Recipe Contest sponsored by the National Sunflower Association, Bismarck, North Dakota.

Makes one 13×9-inch cake

> 4 eggs
> 2 cups granulated sugar
> 2 cups sour cream
> 3 cups all-purpose flour
> 1 teaspoon baking powder
> 1 teaspoon baking soda
> ¼ teaspoon salt
> 1½ cups diced peeled apples
> ½ cup sunflower kernels, toasted
> Topping (recipe follows)
> Whipped cream for garnish (optional)
> Additional toasted sunflower kernels for garnish (optional)

Preheat oven to 350°F. Grease 13×9-inch baking pan. Beat together eggs, sugar and sour cream in large bowl until well blended. Sift together dry ingredients. Add to sugar mixture; mix well. Stir in apples and sunflower kernels. Pour into prepared pan. Sprinkle with Topping. Bake 25 to 30 minutes or until wooden pick inserted in center comes out clean. Serve warm or at room temperature. Garnish as desired.

Topping: Combine ¼ cup (½ stick) softened sunflower margarine and ⅔ cup packed brown sugar, mixing until well blended. Add ⅔ cup all-purpose flour and ½ teaspoon ground cinnamon; mix well. Stir in ½ cup sunflower kernels.

Fruit Cake

♦ Stephanie Gamblin from Albuquerque, New Mexico was a finalist in the Cakes category at the New Mexico State Fair, Albuquerque, New Mexico.

Makes one 9×5-inch loaf

3 cups shelled nuts
2 (4-ounce) packages candied pineapple
1 (8-ounce) package candied cherries
1 (8-ounce) package chopped dates
¾ cup sifted all-purpose flour
¾ cup sugar
½ teaspoon baking powder
½ teaspoon salt
3 eggs, slightly beaten
1 teaspoon vanilla

Preheat oven to 300°F. Line 9×5-inch loaf pan with greased waxed paper. Stir together nuts and fruit in large bowl; set aside. Combine dry ingredients. Sift over nut mixture; toss lightly until nuts and fruit are well coated. Blend in eggs and vanilla. Spread into prepared pan. Bake 1 hour and 45 minutes or until golden brown. Cool completely in pan on wire rack before removing from pan.

POTPOURRI

Old World Walnut Cake

♦ Gayle Wagner from Metairie, Louisiana was a finalist in a cookbook and recipe contest sponsored by *The Times-Picayune*, New Orleans, Louisiana.

Makes one 3-layer cake

Sugar
7 **eggs, separated**
⅔ **cup** *combined* **orange and lemon juice**
2 **tablespoons vanilla, divided**
2 **teaspoons** *combined* **grated orange and lemon peel**
6 **ounces walnuts, ground**
¼ **cup dry bread crumbs**
3½ **pints (7 cups) whipping cream**
Additional whipped cream for garnish (optional)
Additional ground walnuts for garnish (optional)
Orange zest and cherries for garnish (optional)

Preheat oven to 350°F. Grease and flour 3 (8- or 9-inch) round cake pans. Beat together 1 cup sugar and egg yolks in large bowl until well blended. Add juice, 1 tablespoon of the vanilla, the orange and lemon peel, 6 ounces walnuts and bread crumbs. Beat egg whites in separate bowl at high speed with electric mixer until stiff peaks form; fold into sugar mixture. Pour evenly into prepared pans. Bake 25 to 30 minutes or until wooden pick inserted in centers comes out clean. Cool layers in pans on wire racks 10 minutes. Loosen edges and remove to racks to cool completely. Beat whipping cream in separate large bowl at medium speed with electric mixer until soft peaks form. Gradually add the remaining 1 tablespoon vanilla and additional sugar to taste, beating at high speed until stiff peaks form. Fill and frost with whipped cream mixture. Garnish as desired. Refrigerate.

Sour Cream Coffeecake Cupcakes

♦ Marie Bailey from Spencer, West Virginia was a first place winner in the Cupcakes category in the Black Walnut Bake-Off at the Black Walnut Festival, Spencer, West Virginia.

Makes about 1½ dozen cupcakes

    1 cup (2 sticks) butter, softened (*do not use* margarine)
    2 cups plus 4 teaspoons sugar, divided
    2 eggs
    1 cup sour cream
    1 teaspoon vanilla
    2 cups all-purpose flour
    1 teaspoon salt
    ½ teaspoon baking soda
    1 cup chopped black walnuts
    1 teaspoon ground cinnamon

Preheat oven to 350°F. Insert paper liners into 18 muffin cups. Beat together butter and 2 cups of the sugar in large bowl. Add eggs, one at a time, beating well after each addition. Blend in sour cream and vanilla. Combine flour, salt and baking soda; set aside. Add to butter mixture; mix well. Stir together the remaining 4 teaspoons sugar, the walnuts and cinnamon. Fill prepared muffin cups one third full with batter; sprinkle with two thirds of the walnut mixture. Fill cups with remaining batter; sprinkle with remaining walnut mixture. Bake 25 to 30 minutes or until wooden pick inserted into centers comes out clean. Remove cupcakes from pan; cool on wire rack.

Velvety Coconut and Spice Cake

♦ Lisa Groesch from Springfield, Illinois was a finalist in the "Bake-a-Cake" category in the Blue Ribbon Culinary Contest at the Illinois State Fair, Springfield, Illinois.

Makes one 3-layer cake

2½ cups all-purpose flour
1½ teaspoons baking powder
 ¾ teaspoon baking soda
 ½ teaspoon salt
1½ teaspoons ground cinnamon
 ¼ teaspoon ground cloves
 ¼ teaspoon ground nutmeg
 ¼ teaspoon ground allspice
 ¼ teaspoon ground cardamom
 ½ cup (1 stick) butter or margarine, softened
 ½ cup granulated sugar
 ½ cup packed brown sugar
 4 eggs
 1 teaspoon vanilla
1½ cups light cream
 ¼ cup molasses
1½ cups shredded coconut
 ⅔ cup orange marmalade
   Creamy Orange Frosting (recipe follows)
   Toasted coconut for garnish (optional)

Preheat oven to 350°F. Grease 3 (8-inch) round cake pans; sprinkle with enough granulated sugar to lightly coat bottoms and sides of pans. Combine flour, baking powder, baking soda, salt and spices; set aside. Beat butter in large bowl until creamy. Add sugars; beat until light and fluffy. Add eggs, one at a time, beating well after each addition. Blend in vanilla. Combine light cream and molasses. Add flour mixture to egg mixture alternately with molasses mixture, beating well after each addition. Stir in coconut. Pour evenly into prepared pans. Bake 20 minutes or until wooden pick inserted in centers comes out clean. Cool layers in pans on wire racks 10 minutes. Loosen edges and remove to racks to cool completely. To assemble, spread 2 layers with marmalade; stack on cake plate. Top with third layer. Frost with Creamy Orange Frosting. Refrigerate. Garnish as desired.

Creamy Orange Frosting: Beat 1 (3-ounce) package softened cream cheese in large bowl until creamy. Gradually add 2 cups powdered sugar, beating until fluffy. Blend in a few drops orange extract. (Add milk, a teaspoonful at a time, if necessary for desired consistency.)

Brandy-Pecan Corn Meal Cake

♦ Patricia Schroedel from Jefferson, Wisconsin was a first prize winner in the Cakes Category in the Quaker Corn Meal "Contemporary Classics" Recipe Contest sponsored by The Quaker Oats Company, Chicago, Illinois.

Makes one 10-inch tube cake

      1 cup (2 sticks) margarine, softened
   1¼ cups granulated sugar
    ¾ cup packed brown sugar
      5 eggs
      1 cup sour cream
    ½ cup brandy
   2¼ cups all-purpose flour
    ½ cup QUAKER® Enriched Corn Meal
      2 teaspoons baking powder
      1 teaspoon salt (optional)
      1 teaspoon ground cinnamon
    ½ teaspoon ground nutmeg
   1½ cups chopped pecans
         Glaze (recipe follows)
         Pecan halves for garnish (optional)

Preheat oven to 325°F. Generously grease and flour 10-inch fluted tube or tube pan. Beat together margarine and sugars in large bowl until light and fluffy. Add eggs, one at a time, beating well after each addition. Blend in sour cream and brandy. Sift together dry ingredients. Add to margarine mixture, mixing until well blended. Stir in pecans. Pour into prepared pan, spreading evenly to edges. Bake 65 to 70 minutes or until wooden pick inserted in center comes out clean. (Surface will appear slightly wet in center.) Cool in pan on wire rack 10 minutes. Loosen edges and remove to rack to cool completely. Drizzle with Glaze. Garnish as desired. Store tightly covered.

Glaze: Heat 2 tablespoons margarine in medium saucepan over medium heat until melted and golden brown; cool slightly. Add 1 cup powdered sugar, 1 to 2 teaspoons brandy and 4 teaspoons milk, beating until smooth. (Add additional 1 teaspoon milk if necessary for desired consistency.)

Champion Pumpkin Cake

♦ Sharon Jones from Kingston, Ohio was the Grand Champion in the Cakes category at the Circleville Pumpkin Festival, Circleville, Ohio.

Makes one 2-layer cake

- ¾ cup shortening
- 1½ cups granulated sugar
- 3 eggs
- 1½ cups solid-pack pumpkin
- 1 cup buttermilk
- 2¾ cups all-purpose flour
- 1 tablespoon baking powder
- 1½ teaspoons baking soda
- ½ teaspoon salt
- 1 teaspoon ground cinnamon
- ¼ teaspoon ground allspice
- ¼ teaspoon ground nutmeg
- ⅛ teaspoon ground ginger
- ⅛ teaspoon pumpkin pie spice
- Snow Frosting (recipe follows)

Preheat oven to 350°F. Grease and flour 2 (9-inch) round cake pans. Beat together shortening and sugar in large bowl until light and fluffy. Add eggs, one at a time, beating well after each addition. Combine pumpkin and buttermilk. Sift together dry ingredients; add to creamed mixture alternately with pumpkin mixture, beating well after each addition. Pour evenly into prepared pans. Bake 40 to 45 minutes or until wooden pick inserted in centers comes out clean. Cool layers in pans on wire racks 10 minutes. Loosen edges and remove to racks to cool completely. Fill and frost with Snow Frosting.

Snow Frosting: Beat together ½ cup shortening and ½ cup (1 stick) softened butter in large bowl until light and fluffy. Add 2 egg whites* and 1 teaspoon vanilla; mix until well blended. Gradually add 4 cups powdered sugar, beating until light and fluffy.

*Use clean, uncracked eggs.

Kansas Kids' Cake

♦ Deborah Umscheid from Manhattan, Kansas was a contest winner in the Dessert category in the Celebrate! Kansas Food Recipe Contest.

Makes one 13×9-inch cake

½ cup (1 stick) butter, softened
¼ cup peanut butter
¾ cup honey
2 eggs
1 teaspoon vanilla
1 cup all-purpose flour
1 cup whole-wheat flour
1½ teaspoons baking powder
¾ teaspoon baking soda
½ teaspoon salt
¾ cup buttermilk
Topping (recipe follows)

Preheat oven to 350°F. Grease and lightly flour 13×9-inch baking pan. Beat together butter, peanut butter and honey in large bowl until well blended. Blend in eggs and vanilla. Sift together dry ingredients; add to peanut butter mixture alternately with buttermilk, beating well after each addition. Pour into prepared pan. Prepare Topping; crumble over batter. Bake 25 to 30 minutes or until wooden pick inserted in center comes out clean. Serve warm or at room temperature.

Topping: Combine ½ cup peanut butter, ¾ cup sugar and 2 tablespoons all-purpose flour, mixing until well blended. Stir in 1 cup semisweet chocolate chips.

Caramel-Butter Pecan Cake

◆ Joanna Bull from Humnoke, Arkansas was a finalist in the Cakes category at the Arkansas State Fair, Little Rock, Arkansas.

Makes one 3-layer cake

    1 cup shortening
    2 cups granulated sugar
    4 eggs
    3 cups sifted cake flour
 2½ teaspoons baking powder
  ½ teaspoon salt
    1 cup milk
    1 teaspoon vanilla
    1 teaspoon almond extract
      Caramel Filling (recipe follows)
      Butter Cream Frosting (recipe follows)
  ¼ cup chopped pecans

Preheat oven to 350°F. Grease and flour 3 (9-inch) round cake pans. Beat together shortening and sugar in large bowl until light and fluffy. Add eggs, one at a time, beating well after each addition. Sift together dry ingredients. Add to sugar mixture alternately with milk, beating well after each addition. Blend in flavorings. Pour evenly into prepared pans. Bake 20 to 25 minutes or until wooden pick inserted in centers comes out clean. Cool layers in pans on wire racks 10 minutes. Loosen edges and remove to racks to cool completely. To assemble, spread tops of layers with Caramel Filling; stack on cake plate. Spread sides of cake with Butter Cream Frosting. Sprinkle with pecans.

Caramel Filling: Place ½ cup granulated sugar in large heavy saucepan. Cook over medium heat, stirring constantly, until sugar is light golden brown. Combine 2½ cups granulated sugar, ¾ cup milk, 1 beaten egg and dash of salt in medium bowl; stir in ½ cup (1 stick) softened butter. Add to caramelized sugar. Cook over *medium* heat, stirring occasionally, until candy thermometer registers 230°F (15 to 20 minutes); cool 5 minutes. Stir with wooden spoon until well blended and thickened.

Butter Cream Frosting: Beat ⅓ cup (⅔ stick) softened butter in large bowl until creamy. Gradually add 3 cups sifted powdered sugar alternately with 2 tablespoons half and half, beating until light and fluffy. (Add additional 1 tablespoon half and half if necessary for desired consistency.) Stir in ½ teaspoon vanilla.

Sweet Potato Cake

♦ Donna V. Leeson from New Orleans, Louisiana was a finalist in a cookbook and recipe contest sponsored by *The Times-Picayune*, New Orleans, Louisiana.

Makes one 3-layer cake

   2 cups sugar
1½ cups vegetable oil
   4 eggs, separated
¼ cup water
2½ cups all-purpose flour
   1 tablespoon baking powder
¼ teaspoon salt
1¼ teaspoons ground cinnamon
½ teaspoon ground ginger
½ teaspoon ground nutmeg
¼ teaspoon ground cloves
1½ cups shredded sweet potato
   1 cup chopped pecans
   1 teaspoon vanilla
      Coconut Filling (recipe follows)
      Pecan halves and flaked coconut for garnish
      (optional)

Preheat oven to 350°F. Grease and flour 3 (8-inch) round cake pans. Beat together sugar and oil in large bowl until smooth. Add egg yolks, beating until well blended. Blend in water. Sift together dry ingredients. Add to sugar mixture; mix well. Stir in sweet potato, pecans and vanilla. Beat egg whites in separate bowl at high speed with electric mixer until stiff peaks form; fold into batter. Pour evenly into prepared pans. Bake 25 to 30 minutes or until wooden pick inserted in centers comes out clean. Cool layers in pans on wire racks 10 minutes. Loosen edges and remove to racks to cool completely. To assemble, spread layers with Coconut Filling; stack on cake plate. Garnish as desired.

Coconut Filling: Combine 1 (13-ounce) can evaporated milk, 1 cup sugar, ½ cup (1 stick) softened butter, 3 tablespoons all-purpose flour and 1½ teaspoons vanilla in saucepan. Cook, stirring constantly, over medium heat 10 to 12 minutes or until thickened. Remove from heat; stir in 1½ cups flaked coconut and ½ cup chopped pecans. Beat until thickened and cooled.

DECADENT CHEESECAKES

Turtle Pecan Cheesecake

◆ Linda Bland from Edwardsville, Illinois was a finalist in the Baked Desserts Using Dairy Products category at the Illinois State Fair, Springfield, Illinois.

Makes one 9-inch cheesecake

    2 cups crushed chocolate cookies or vanilla wafers
        (approximately 8 ounces cookies)
    ¼ cup (½ stick) butter, melted
    2½ (8-ounce) packages cream cheese, softened
    1 cup sugar
    1½ tablespoons all-purpose flour
    ¼ teaspoon salt
    1 teaspoon vanilla
    3 eggs
    2 tablespoons whipping cream
      Caramel Topping (recipe follows)
      Chocolate Topping (recipe follows)
    1 cup chopped toasted pecans

Preheat oven to 450°F. Combine cookie crumbs and butter; press onto bottom of 9-inch springform pan. Beat cream cheese in large bowl until creamy. Add sugar, flour, salt and vanilla; mix well. Add eggs, one at a time, beating well after each addition. Blend in cream. Pour over crust. Bake 10 minutes. *Reduce oven temperature to 200°F*; continue baking 35 to 40 minutes or until set. Loosen cake from rim of pan; cool before removing rim of pan. Drizzle with Caramel Topping and Chocolate Topping. Refrigerate. Sprinkle with pecans just before serving.

Caramel Topping: Combine ½ (14-ounce) bag caramels and ⅓ cup whipping cream in small saucepan; stir over low heat until smooth.

Chocolate Topping: Combine 1 (4-ounce) package German sweet chocolate, 1 teaspoon butter and 2 tablespoons whipping cream in small saucepan; stir over low heat until smooth.

Gourmet Gala Cheesecake with Orange Rum Sauce

♦ Eleanor Ostman and Ron Aune entered this prize-winning recipe at the March of Dimes Gourmet Gala in Minneapolis, Minnesota.

Makes one 10-inch cheesecake

    4 (8-ounce) packages cream cheese, softened
  ½ cup (1 stick) butter, softened
    2 cups (16 ounces) sour cream
1¼ cups sugar
    2 tablespoons cornstarch
    2 teaspoons lemon juice
    1 teaspoon vanilla
    5 eggs, at room temperature
      Orange Rum Sauce (recipe follows)

Preheat oven to 375°F. Thoroughly grease 10-inch springform pan. Beat together cream cheese and butter in large bowl until creamy. Blend in sour cream. Add sugar, cornstarch, lemon juice and vanilla; beat until well blended. Add eggs, one at a time, beating well after each addition. Pour into prepared pan. Place springform pan in a larger pan; add enough water to come halfway up outside of springform pan. Bake 1 hour or until set. Turn off oven. Let cheesecake cool in oven 1 hour with oven door slightly open. Remove cheesecake from oven; let stand on wire rack 2 hours. Loosen cake from rim of pan; cool completely before removing rim of pan. Refrigerate at least 6 hours before serving. Serve with Orange Rum Sauce.

Orange Rum Sauce: Using a zester or vegetable peeler, remove only orange portion of peel from each of 3 oranges. Cut into very thin slivers to make ½ cup. Squeeze juice from oranges; strain. (There should be enough juice to make 1 cup. If necessary, add enough water to juice to measure 1 cup.) Place juice and orange peel in small saucepan; simmer over low heat 5 minutes. Add ½ cup corn syrup, ¼ cup sugar and ¼ cup dark rum; stir until the sugar dissolves. Increase heat to high; bring to a boil. Reduce heat to medium; boil 20 minutes or until liquid becomes syrupy. Remove from heat; cool thoroughly. Stir in ¼ cup chopped macadamia nuts.

Chocolate Amaretto Cheesecake

♦ Bob McCabe from Minneapolis-St. Paul, Minnesota was a prize winner in the Dessert category in the LAND O' LAKES® Employee Sales Recipe Contest sponsored by Land O' Lakes, Inc., Minneapolis, Minnesota.

Makes one 9-inch cheesecake

1½ cups finely crushed chocolate wafer cookies
 1 cup chopped almonds
1⅓ cups sugar, divided
 6 tablespoons LAND O' LAKES® Country Morning Blend, softened
 3 (8-ounce) packages cream cheese, softened
 4 eggs
⅓ cup whipping cream
¼ cup almond-flavored liqueur
 1 teaspoon vanilla
 Topping (recipe follows)
 Toasted sliced almonds for garnish (optional)

Preheat oven to 350°F. Grease bottom and sides of 9-inch springform pan. Combine crumbs, almonds and ⅓ cup of the sugar in medium bowl. Cut in margarine-butter blend until mixture resembles coarse crumbs. Press onto bottom and sides of prepared pan. Beat together the remaining 1 cup sugar and the cream cheese in large bowl until smooth and creamy. Add eggs, one at a time, beating well after each addition. Blend in whipping cream, liqueur and vanilla. Pour into crust. Bake 40 to 45 minutes or until firm to the touch. Let stand on wire rack 5 minutes. Meanwhile, prepare Topping; carefully spread over cheesecake. Return cheesecake to oven; continue baking 5 minutes. Loosen cake from rim of pan; cool before removing rim of pan. Refrigerate. Garnish as desired.

Topping: Combine 2 cups LAND O' LAKES® Light Sour Cream Dairy Blend or Sour Cream, 1 tablespoon sugar and 1 teaspoon vanilla, mixing until well blended.

Apple Cheesecake

♦ Cynthia Donnay from Oak Park, Michigan was a finalist in the Public Category at the Apple Cooking Contest sponsored by the Michigan Apple Committee, De Witt, Michigan.

Makes one 9-inch cheesecake

    1 cup graham cracker crumbs
      Sugar
    1 teaspoon ground cinnamon, divided
    3 tablespoons margarine, melted
    2 (8-ounce) packages cream cheese, softened
    2 eggs
    ½ teaspoon vanilla
    4 cups peeled, thin apple slices (about 2½ pounds
        apples)
    ½ cup chopped pecans

Preheat oven to 350°F. Combine crumbs, 3 tablespoons sugar, ½ teaspoon of the cinnamon and the margarine; press onto bottom and sides of 9-inch pie plate. Bake 10 minutes. Beat together cream cheese and ½ cup sugar in large bowl until well blended. Add eggs, one at a time, beating well after each addition. Blend in vanilla; pour into crust. Toss apples with combined ⅓ cup sugar and the remaining ½ teaspoon cinnamon. Spoon over cream cheese mixture; sprinkle with pecans. Bake 1 hour and 10 minutes or until set. Loosen cake from rim of pan; cool before removing rim of pan. Refrigerate.

Supreme Chocolate Cheesecake

♦ Kim Marsden from Renton, Washington was a winner in the "PHILLY"® Hall of Fame Recipe Contest sponsored by PHILADELPHIA BRAND® Cream Cheese, Glenview, Illinois.

Makes one 9-inch cheesecake

16 chocolate sandwich cookies, crushed (about 1½ cups)
¼ cup (½ stick) PARKAY® Margarine, melted
 3 (8-ounce) packages PHILADELPHIA BRAND® Cream Cheese, softened
 1 (14-ounce) can sweetened condensed milk
 3 eggs
 1 (12-ounce) package BAKER'S® Semi-Sweet Real Chocolate Chips, melted
 2 teaspoons vanilla
   Topping (recipe follows)
   Additional chocolate sandwich cookies for garnish (optional)
   Orange slices and orange zest for garnish (optional)

Preheat oven to 300°F. Combine cookie crumbs and margarine; press onto bottom of 9-inch springform pan. Set aside. Beat together cream cheese and milk in large bowl until well blended. Add eggs, one at a time, beating well after each addition. Blend in chocolate and vanilla. Pour over crust. Bake 1 hour and 10 minutes. Loosen cake from rim of pan; cool before removing rim of pan. Spread Topping over top and sides of cheesecake. Refrigerate. Let stand at room temperature 30 minutes before serving. Garnish as desired.

Topping: Beat together ⅓ cup (⅔ stick) softened PARKAY® Margarine and ½ cup powdered sugar in small bowl until light and fluffy. Add 1 cup (6 ounces) BAKER'S® Semi-Sweet Real Chocolate Chips, melted and cooled, and 2 tablespoons orange-flavored liqueur, mixing until well blended.

Orange Cappuccino Cheesecake

◆ Shirley Britt from Lincoln, Illinois was a finalist in the Baked Desserts Using Dairy Products category at the Illinois State Fair, Springfield, Illinois.

Makes one 9-inch cheescake

1½ cups finely chopped nuts
1 cup plus 2 tablespoons sugar, divided
3 tablespoons butter, melted
4 (8-ounce) packages cream cheese, softened
3 tablespoons all-purpose flour
4 eggs
1 cup sour cream
1 tablespoon instant coffee powder
¼ teaspoon ground cinnamon
¼ cup orange juice
1 teaspoon grated orange peel
Cinnamon sugar for garnish (optional)
Whipped cream and orange zest for garnish
(optional)

Preheat oven to 325°F. Combine nuts, 2 tablespoons of the sugar and the butter; press onto bottom of 9-inch springform pan. Bake 10 minutes. Remove from oven. *Increase oven temperature to 450°F.* Beat together cream cheese, the remaining 1 cup sugar and the flour in large bowl until well blended. Add eggs, one at a time, beating well after each addition. Blend in sour cream. Add coffee powder and cinnamon to orange juice; stir until coffee is dissolved. Gradually add juice mixture with orange peel to cream cheese mixture, mixing until well blended. Pour over crust. Bake 10 minutes. *Reduce oven temperature to 250°F;* continue baking 1 hour. Loosen cake from rim of pan; cool before removing rim of pan. Refrigerate. Sprinkle top of cheesecake with cinnamon sugar, if desired. Garnish as desired.

Lemon Dream Cheesecake

♦ Allan S. Levine from New Orleans, Louisiana was a first prize winner in the Desserts and Candy category in a cookbook and recipe contest sponsored by *The Times Picayune*, New Orleans, Louisiana.

Makes one 9-inch cheesecake

- **1 cup graham cracker crumbs**
- **1 cup ground pecans**
- **6 tablespoons butter, melted**
- **¾ cup plus 2 tablespoons sugar, divided**
- **1 tablespoon plus 2 teaspoons coffee-flavored liqueur, divided**
- **3 (8-ounce) packages cream cheese, softened**
- **3 eggs**
- **¼ cup lemon juice**
- **2 teaspoons grated lemon peel**
- **2 teaspoons vanilla**
  Topping (recipe follows)
  Lemon Glaze (recipe follows)
  Kiwifruit and strawberries for garnish (optional)

Preheat oven to 350°F. Combine crumbs, pecans, butter, 2 tablespoons of the sugar and 1 tablespoon of the coffee-flavored liqueur; press onto bottom and sides of 9-inch springform pan. Bake 5 minutes. Beat cream cheese in large bowl until creamy. Add the remaining ¾ cup sugar, mixing until well blended. Add eggs, one at a time, beating well after each addition. Blend in the remaining 2 teaspoons coffee-flavored liqueur, the lemon juice, lemon peel and vanilla. Pour into crust. Bake 35 minutes. Remove cheesecake from oven; carefully spoon Topping over cheesecake. Return cheesecake to oven; continue baking 12 minutes or until set. Cool 30 minutes. Meanwhile, prepare Lemon Glaze; let cool. Loosen cake from rim of pan; cool before removing rim of pan. Top cooled cheesecake with cooled Lemon Glaze. Garnish as desired.

Topping: Combine 2 cups sour cream, 3 tablespoons sugar, 1 teaspoon vanilla and 1 teaspoon coffee-flavored liqueur, mixing until well blended.

Lemon Glaze: Combine ½ cup sugar, 1½ tablespoons cornstarch and ¼ teaspoon salt in saucepan. Add combined ¾ cup water, ⅓ cup lemon juice and 1 beaten egg yolk. Cook over low heat, stirring constantly, until mixture starts to boil and is thickened. Stir in 1 tablespoon butter and 1 teaspoon grated lemon peel.

White Chocolate Cheesecake

♦ Gloria Pleasants from Williamsburg, Virginia was a first place winner in the Cheesecake category in the "PHILLY"® Hall of Fame Recipe Contest sponsored by PHILADELPHIA BRAND® Cream Cheese, Glenview, Illinois.

Makes one 9-inch cheesecake

1½ cups all-purpose flour
½ cup granulated sugar
½ cup (1 stick) PARKAY® Margarine
½ cup finely chopped toasted almonds or macadamia nuts
4 (1-ounce) squares white baking chocolate, grated
4 eggs, divided
8 (1-ounce) squares white baking chocolate, chopped
⅓ cup whipping cream
1 tablespoon vanilla
3 (8-ounce) packages PHILADELPHIA BRAND® Cream Cheese, softened
1 (14-ounce) can sweetened condensed milk
Powdered sugar for garnish (optional)
Additional grated white chocolate and toasted sliced almonds for garnish (optional)
Strawberries for garnish (optional)

Preheat oven to 325°F. Stir together flour and granulated sugar in small bowl; cut in margarine until mixture resembles coarse crumbs. Add almonds, grated chocolate and 1 beaten egg, mixing until well blended. Press onto bottom and sides of 9-inch springform pan. Chill. Stir together chopped chocolate and whipping cream in double boiler; cook, stirring constantly, over simmering water until chocolate is melted. Stir in vanilla; keep warm. Beat together cream cheese and milk in medium bowl until well blended. Add the remaining 3 eggs, one at a time, beating well after each addition. Stir in chocolate mixture. Pour over crust. Bake 1 hour and 20 minutes or until set. Loosen cake from rim of pan; cool before removing rim of pan. Chill. Dust lightly with powdered sugar just before serving, if desired. Garnish as desired.

INDEX